Adam Wants, Adam Needs

Zvika Bakshi | Nina Dar

Illustrated by Naama Lahav

Translated from Hebrew by N.Kaspi

"Please, Mom and Dad, I need this one the most!"
said Adam, while munching on a slice of toast.
"I've got the same car model in blue,
but I really want it in purple, too!"

Mom turned to Adam, a kind look in her eyes,
and said in a voice both patient and wise:
"There's a difference between need and want, my child.
"Now, let me explain," she added, and smiled.

"When Toffee the dog runs to the front door,
so eager to walk and can't wait anymore.
What do you think, as he whimpers and pleads?
Is a walk something he wants or needs?"

"He needs it," said Adam, without any doubt.
"To go to the toilet, he must be let out."

"And what about Eden, your sister? You know,
how each morning she watches her favorite show?
Does she want it or need it, what would you say?
Is this something she must do every day?"

"Of course, it's just something she wants to do.
Hey! I can think logically, just like you!
I've never played this game before.
Please mom, can you ask me a few more?"

"Sure, how about brushing your teeth before bed,
though you'd rather play a bit longer instead?"

"Simple – that's something I need to do.
Please ask me some more, mom, just a few!"

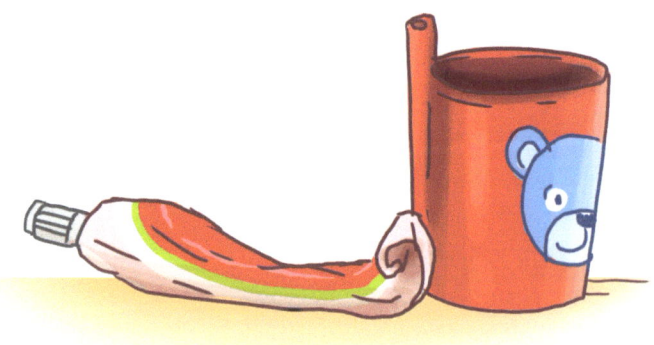

"If this is so simple, I have a suggestion:
Let me ask you a slightly more difficult question.
You will need to think for a moment or two,
before you tell me which one is true.

When your mother and father go to work every day,
do they want to go out or would they rather stay?"
asked Mom, and let Adam think and grapple,
while she waited and peeled herself an apple.

"This shouldn't really be that complicated,"
said Adam, unsure, but then boldly stated:
"Everyone knows – work is not funny.
It's what people do to earn their money."

"Let me tell you a secret, my clever one:
Work can be sometimes a lot of fun.
We create and produce and even socialize.
Work may be more exciting than you realize."

"That's true," said Dad, "work is need and want, too.
Is it OK if I join you two?"

"What do you think of our shoes and our clothes?
Can we survive without either of those?"
asked Dad and poured water into his glass.
"I wonder what kind of judgment you'll pass…"

"Of course we can't, Dad!" Adam quickly replied,
and looked at his father, beaming with pride.

"And an apple, a carrot or maybe a cake?
Tomato, potato, and an ice-cold milkshake?"

For a moment, Adam seemed confused.
Then he turned to his mother, rather bemused:
"A trick question! But let me try:
A cake is a treat, and so is a pie.
But there is absolutely no substitute,
for healthy slices of vegetables and fruit!"

"That's fantastic, sweetheart, now just two more.
Let's see if you can do as well as before.

When Toffee brings you his favorite ball
and barks his usual 'come on!' call,
what do you think he is trying to say?
Can you imagine why he's acting that way?"

"Of course I can, Mom, I know Toffee so well.
He is my best friend - I can easily tell.
Fetching is what he loves most of all,
especially when I throw his favorite ball."

"That's true, my darling, so now pay attention:
What about the new purple car you've mentioned?
Isn't it also a wonderful toy,
meant for you to play and enjoy?"

"Mom, you're so clever, I understand now.
Thank you for showing me exactly how
the difference between want and need
is a very interesting problem indeed.
'Is what I want something I can do without?'
This question is what it is all about."

Everyone can sometimes think of these questions,
and whether we want or need new possessions.
Boys and girls, you could try it, too –
thinking like grownups is a cool thing to do!

"And now, Mom and Dad – one riddle for you,"
said Adam, "which of these options is true?
Think of your answer if you want to succeed:
Is my cuddle something you want, or need?"

Adam Wants, Adam Needs
Zvika Bakshi | Nina Dar

Illustrated by Naama Lahav
Edited (Hebrew) by Efrat Eckshtein
Translated from Hebrew by: N. Kaspi
Designed by Batya Eisen
©Michaeli Financial Education Ltd.

www.funfinance.co.il
funfinance1@gmail.com
+972-506001060

About FunFinance

FunFinance is a unique financial education program for young children, taught throughout the country. Participants acquire the knowledge and tools for understanding real-life financial concepts: effective financial management, clever consumerism, business planning, and the benefits of saving; all while considering the needs of their family and community. The program provides more than theoretic knowledge, it also covers learning strategies and practical tools that help young students develop a 'financial intelligence' and make informed decisions from a young age.

Michaeli – Financial Education Ltd is the first and leading Israeli provider of financial education for young children.
The company invests substantial resources in the development of high-quality content for the benefit of its participants.

Zvika Bakshi is the Company's founder and the FunFinance brand developer. An expert in knowledge management, Bakshi has a master's degree with distinction from the Bar-Ilan University and lectures on Finance and Competitive Intelligence.

Nina Dar is a medical doctor and children's writer who has a degree in Neuroscience from Tel Aviv University. Her first book was selected for the Books with Meaning project, and its English version is currently sold at various bookstores, including Amazon.

All rights reserved. No part of this publication may be reproduced, stored in a retrieval system, or transmitted in any form by any means (electronic, mechanical, photocopying, recording or otherwise) without the prior written permission of the publisher.

www.ingramcontent.com/pod-product-compliance
Lightning Source LLC
Chambersburg PA
CBHW051834210526
45473CB00005B/1874